PRACTICAL STUFF FOR PASTORS

DEALING WITH CONFLICT

Loveland, CO

Group
Real. **Bold**. Love.

Group resources actually work!

This Group resource incorporates our R.E.A.L. approach to ministry. It reinforces a growing friendship with Jesus, encourages long-term learning, and results in life transformation, because it's

Relational
Learner-to-learner interaction enhances learning and builds Christian friendships.

Experiential
What learners experience through discussion and action sticks with them up to 9 times longer than what they simply hear or read.

Applicable
The aim of Christian education is to equip learners to be both hearers and doers of God's Word.

Learner-based
Learners understand and retain more when the learning process takes into consideration how they learn best.

PRACTICAL STUFF FOR PASTORS:
DEALING WITH CONFLICT

Visit our website: **group.com**

Credits
Editor: Rick Edwards
Assistant Editor: Kelsey Perry
Art and Design: Amy Taylor, Andy Towler
Contributing Authors: Jeremy Amick, Susan Lawrence, Mark Lail, Austin Maxheimer, Tony Myles, Larry Shallenberger, Brian Walton

Unless otherwise indicated, all Scripture quotations are taken from the *Holy Bible*, New Living Translation, copyright © 1996, 2004, 2007, 2013 by Tyndale House Foundation. Used by permission of Tyndale House Publishers, Inc., Carol Stream, Illinois 60188. All rights reserved.

ISBN 978-1-4707-2070-4

Printed in the United States of America.

10 9 8 7 6 5 4 3 2 1   24 23 22 21 20 19 18 17 16 15

CONTENTS

INTRODUCTION

You may not need this book.

That is, you won't need it if you're looking for a rhetorical analysis of Paul's speech on Mars Hill. You learned how to use Bible commentaries in college or seminary.

You don't need this book if you want to describe the different historical interpretations of the presence of Christ in the Lord's Supper. Church history class covered that.

Nor will this book help you identify the appropriate developmental stage children should be at before teaching them the story of David and Bathsheba. If you really don't know that, maybe it's time to take a teacher or a parent out for coffee.

When we at Group Publishing wondered what kind of resource we could offer to pastors, we asked hundreds of pastors what they wish they'd learned in seminary, but didn't. The overwhelming response was "practical stuff." This book is our response.

Practical Stuff for Pastors is a series of handbooks dedicated to topics such as how to manage a team, handle property and financial issues, diffuse conflicts, lead change, and more. We've assembled a team of pastors, church leaders, and business professionals who provide tips, recommendations, and strategies for the practical responsibilities pastors deal with on a regular basis.

PRACTICAL STUFF FOR PASTORS:
DEALING WITH CONFLICT

In keeping with this book's practical approach, you'll find that the table of contents doubles as a topical index. The plain, straightforward chapter titles don't try to be clever, but clearly describe the topic they address. The stand-alone chapters can be read in any sequence, at any time you need to access them. The writing style is informal, with easy, accessible language; and we used mostly short words.

So whenever you need to look up how to do some practical ministry stuff:

- Look up your topic in the table of contents.
- Read the chapter.
- Act on what you read: make a call, plan a meeting, create a job description, or delegate a task.

Dealing With Conflict

This volume of Practical Stuff for Pastors focuses on conflict—how to recognize it, when and how to avoid it, when *not* to avoid it, and what to do about it. Conflict in the church has a unique character not usually encountered in the average home or workplace. In those settings conflict is pretty much expected. Churches aren't supposed to have conflict; we're all Christians, aren't we? Christians are all perfect and live peacefully together in one accord, right?

Of course, we know that's not true, but still churches have a difficult time acknowledging and dealing with conflict. The chapters in this book will help pastors and church leaders come to grips with various types of conflict in ways that are honest, effective, and biblically sound. Regarding this last descriptor, one of the key biblical passages related to conflict is found in the Gospel of Matthew, chapter 18. Several of our authors refer to it and use it as a framework for dealing with church conflict today. So we have printed it in the Introduction as a handy reference. As you use this book, let Jesus' teachings percolate through your mind and heart and actions so the Holy Spirit can enable you to be a minister of God's reconciling grace.

Matthew 18

¹ About that time the disciples came to Jesus and asked, "Who is greatest in the Kingdom of Heaven?"

² Jesus called a little child to him and put the child among them. ³ Then he said, "I tell you the truth, unless you turn from your sins and become like little children, you will never get into the Kingdom of Heaven. ⁴ So anyone who becomes as humble as this little child is the greatest in the Kingdom of Heaven.

⁵ "And anyone who welcomes a little child like this on my behalf is welcoming me. ⁶ But if you cause one of these little ones who trusts in me to fall into sin, it would be better for you to have a large millstone tied around your neck and be drowned in the depths of the sea.

⁷ "What sorrow awaits the world, because it tempts people to sin. Temptations are inevitable, but what sorrow awaits the person who does the tempting. ⁸ So if your hand or foot causes you to sin, cut it off and throw it away. It's better to enter eternal life with only one hand or one foot than to be thrown into eternal fire with both of your hands and feet. ⁹ And if your eye causes you to sin, gouge it out and throw it away. It's better to enter eternal life with only one eye than to have two eyes and be thrown into the fire of hell.

¹⁰ "Beware that you don't look down on any of these little ones. For I tell you that in heaven their angels are always in the presence of my heavenly Father.

¹² "If a man has a hundred sheep and one of them wanders away, what will he do? Won't he leave the ninety-nine others on the hills and go out to search for the one that is lost? ¹³ And if he finds it, I tell you the truth, he will rejoice over it more than over the ninety-nine that didn't wander away! ¹⁴ In the same way, it is not my heavenly Father's will that even one of these little ones should perish.

¹⁵ "If another believer sins against you, go privately and point out the offense. If the other person listens and confesses it, you have won that person back. ¹⁶ But if you are unsuccessful, take one or two others with you and go back again, so that everything you say may be confirmed by two or three witnesses. ¹⁷ If the person still refuses to listen, take your case to the church. Then if he or she won't accept the church's decision, treat that person as a pagan or a corrupt tax collector.

¹⁸ "I tell you the truth, whatever you forbid on earth will be forbidden in heaven, and whatever you permit on earth will be permitted in heaven.

¹⁹ "I also tell you this: If two of you agree here on earth concerning anything you ask, my Father in heaven will do it for you. ²⁰ For where two or three gather together as my followers, I am there among them."

²¹ Then Peter came to him and asked, "Lord, how often should I forgive someone who sins against me? Seven times?"

PRACTICAL STUFF FOR PASTORS:
DEALING WITH CONFLICT

22 "No, not seven times," Jesus replied, "but seventy times seven!

23 "Therefore, the Kingdom of Heaven can be compared to a king who decided to bring his accounts up to date with servants who had borrowed money from him. 24 In the process, one of his debtors was brought in who owed him millions of dollars. 25 He couldn't pay, so his master ordered that he be sold—along with his wife, his children, and everything he owned—to pay the debt.

26 "But the man fell down before his master and begged him, 'Please, be patient with me, and I will pay it all.' 27 Then his master was filled with pity for him, and he released him and forgave his debt.

28 "But when the man left the king, he went to a fellow servant who owed him a few thousand dollars. He grabbed him by the throat and demanded instant payment.

29 "His fellow servant fell down before him and begged for a little more time. 'Be patient with me, and I will pay it,' he pleaded. 30 But his creditor wouldn't wait. He had the man arrested and put in prison until the debt could be paid in full.

31 "When some of the other servants saw this, they were very upset. They went to the king and told him everything that had happened. 32 Then the king called in the man he had forgiven and said, 'You evil servant! I forgave you that tremendous debt because you pleaded with me. 33 Shouldn't you have mercy on your fellow

servant, just as I had mercy on you?' 34 Then the angry king sent the man to prison to be tortured until he had paid his entire debt.

35 "That's what my heavenly Father will do to you if you refuse to forgive your brothers and sisters from your heart."

RECOGNIZING RED FLAGS

What are the best indicators that a problem is brewing? When you see one, what should you do? When is it better to quietly watch, and when do you need to quickly confront the issue? How can you understand the way conflict works so you don't get easily frustrated and overwhelmed? This chapter can help you answer these questions.

The Process of Conflict

Conflict is not completely predictable. However, knowing the signs of escalating conflict can help you assess where you are and how urgent it is to address the conflict.

1. Unaware. Early in the conflict process, most people won't be aware something is brewing. The seeds of conflict are planted; something is said or neglected, but no one has actually taken offense or established sides.

2. Perceived. Next, the people involved vaguely assess the situation. There is tension, but it hasn't gotten too personal or spread too far.

3. Felt. This third stage affects individuals the most. A few people know why they feel the way they do because they're personally affected. Most people might not know what is going on, but there are feelings of unrest or discontent.

4. **Open.** Finally, conflict is out in the open. More people become aware. Those who tend to avoid conflict disengage. Others jump in and try to determine who is right, how they can fix it, or which side to choose.

5. **Aftermath.** Once the conflict is over, results will vary. Sometimes the aftermath is a jumbled mess of wreckage. Because people were disrespected or ignored, relationships are mangled. Casualties are high, and the healing process is long and costly. Some people walk away in the aftermath. Other times, the issue is resolved, and relationships are stronger because they've weathered the storm together. They shared their perspectives, worked on a solution, and rebuilt something that is stronger than before.

Knowledge of the conflict process is the map that lays out the destination and the general route that must be taken. Before starting the journey, though, you must be able to recognize the mile markers along the way, so you can locate yourself on the map. For church conflicts, you need to be looking for red flags that alert you to danger zones.

Red Flags That Conflict Is Coming

No two conflicts are exactly the same. No single red flag is a guarantee that conflict is coming. You might see a combination of factors or one red flag that is powerful enough to indicate a firestorm ahead. When you keep these warning signs in the back of your mind, you'll connect the dots earlier in the conflict process and be able to address issues more quickly.

- **Consistently longer meetings.** Long meetings might simply indicate many agenda items or inefficient meeting management. However, when meetings consistently get longer, drawn out, and draining, it might be a sign of discontentment, which can quickly lead to conflict.

- **Quiet disunity among leaders or volunteers.** Sometimes things seem to go well during meetings, and the minutes reflect general consensus. However, when informal "meetings after the meeting" grow longer and more frequent, there is cause for concern. Support for dissenting opinions may quietly snowball until they become the main topic of conversations in and out of official meetings and committees.

When informal "meetings after the meeting" grow longer and more frequent, there is cause for concern.

- **Lack of focus.** When leaders spend their time maintaining status quo, conflict is often brewing under the surface. It might take a while to see problems because most people like the relaxed coasting process. Eventually, someone will see the need to change and develop the courage to question the way things are going.

- **A buzz of whispers.** Everyone seems fine when they personally speak to you, but you notice glances and whispers. People begin to avoid you. Bad sign.

- **Repeated questions and phrases.** As people gather support for their cause, they repeat the same conversations with a variety of people. In your conversations with individuals, you'll notice many of them using the same phrases or asking the same questions. This is a sure sign a small group of people have been stirring up others' support and discontentment.

- **Wide-open back door.** It's normal to lose a few people and families from time to time. However, when you see a sudden increase in people leaving, including those who have been committed for a long time, you need to follow up and ask questions as to what issues they might have been experiencing.

- **Key volunteers step aside.** Some might tell you why they are resigning, while people who prefer to avoid conflict will quietly step down. Transitions are ongoing, but when there are spikes of resignations, be sure to investigate.

What Should You Do?

Sometimes you'll need to quietly investigate the murmurings of conflict. Other times you'll need to have open conversations with key people involved. No matter which red flag you see, you should always keep communication open and honest. Be approachable. Ask questions. Invite authenticity. The best defense against conflict is to build relationships before conflict arises. When you have previously established rapport and respect, people will respond better to misunderstandings, accusations, and conflict. People treasure relationships, so they will try to resolve problems in ways that keep relationships intact. Whatever you do, seek God's guidance for discernment.

> The best defense against conflict is to build relationships when there is little to no conflict. When you have previously established rapport and respect, people will respond better to misunderstandings, accusations, and conflict.

Red Flags of Conflict Avoidance

Some churches try to avoid conflict by taking one of the following approaches—all of which, ironically, should be avoided:

Reducing decisions to the lowest common denominator.
When an issue ignites, some leaders will try to keep the majority happy by following the path of least

resistance. Although making decisions based on what will avoid the most conflict might let you breathe for a moment, it reveals a lack of courage in your leadership. When you're not willing to stand up and address issues, people's trust in and respect for you will lessen.

Following the most powerful vote. When you consider the person or group of people who carry the most influence or have the loudest voices, you might be tempted to choose their side and let them carry the burden of the argument. If it's clearly the right choice that will honor God, do it. If you're taking the easy way out, it's not the right choice.

Letting money influence your response. Money is powerful, but it's not a good kind of power. Don't fall into the trap of letting money control your decisions. Revisit Jesus' teachings on the love of money. If donations begin to drop from a large number of givers, you might need to reconsider your own position in case you might be in the wrong. If, on the other hand, you take a stand that causes one or a few people to stop donating—even if they were large givers—find comfort in choosing well and trust God to provide in other ways.

Being content with complacency. If you find comfort in the status quo, you might be finding contentment in the wrong place. Complacency is the overworked soil that produces nothing and fosters no growth. You might avoid conflict, but it's not because of your wise leadership; it's because you're creating a wide path on which just about everything is okay.

The Green Flag of Conflict

Red flags, then, are not to help you avoid conflict. In fact, some conflict may not be all bad. Tension can spur learning and growth. Conflict encourages questions, which leads us to dig into God's Word and clarify faith. Conflict can build relationships when we focus more on people than on an issue. Conflict engages people and keeps the conversation going. It's not comfortable, and it can end poorly. But when conflict is handled well and people are respected during the process, the aftermath can be a powerful testimony to the resiliency of people who honor each other and God above all.

By Susan Lawrence

HANDLING PRICKLY PEOPLE

Control freaks, passive-aggressives, rebels. They all have something in common: they're challenging. They seem to occupy more of your time than everyone else combined. You wonder if you should engage them, ignore them, or redirect them. Whether you have an individual personality conflict with someone or someone is negatively impacting a group, you need tools for dealing with prickly people. As you learn how to deal with these three difficult personalities, you can use the tips to deal with a much wider variety of prickly people.

Control Freaks

Control freaks are those people who seem to be involved in everything. If they're not in charge, they're sharing their opinions. They thrive on input and control. Involvement is a good thing, but if the same people are in charge of just about everything, others are deprived of participation. It isn't a wise use of all the gifts and talents God gives to the church.

How should you deal with control freaks? Wrestle away their power? Limit their involvement? Find someone more powerful to take charge? Ignore them? No. No. No. And no. The best way to deal with control freaks is with respect, combined with mercy and love.

Pray for the person. It's not about praying for *your* will, asking God to change the person. Instead, ask God to give you wisdom for interacting with the person. And be open to the possibility that God's transformative grace will be at work in your life as well.

Build a relationship outside of team meetings and serving together. If all you talk about is "business," you miss out on a level of personal trust and familiarity that may give you insight into the "why" behind his or her attitude and behavior. Getting to know this person better will increase your credibility within the relationship.

Encourage new ways to try things. Instead of pointing out what someone is doing wrong, give ideas of how to include others. You might say something like, "Let's give everyone an opportunity to share. We don't want to put others on the spot and make them uncomfortable, but let's create an environment where everyone feels welcome."

Watch for patterns. Do control tendencies come out under certain circumstances, such as busy, stressful times? One small adjustment that can help is to change seating arrangements. When people sit in the same places over and over, they (and the process) tend to get "stuck" in the same behaviors.

Passive-Aggressives

Passive-aggressiveness is a relationship-killer. Passive-aggressive people...

…try to avoid by selectively forgetting or making last minute excuses.

…conceal or deny their true thoughts and feelings. *"I'm not mad"* (when they are).

…prefer their own agendas while appearing as if they're willing to cooperate with others. *"Fine. Whatever you want. I'm not going to argue"* (with sarcasm, because really, it's not fine).

…don't mind being the cause of the delay but are indignant when someone else causes a delay.

…blame. Instead of accepting personal responsibility, they displace the responsibility onto others and want them to be held accountable.

…play the victim. They compare themselves to others who are in perceived "better" circumstances and positions.

…pretend the issue is not important to them, so they give in or go silent. *"I'll never bring it up again"* (which is really an attempt to punish those with whom they disagree by cutting off all communication).

…frequently complain about being unappreciated and misunderstood by others, but rarely complain to the people who annoy them the most.

…regularly criticize people in authority. They're confident they could do a much better job if they were in the same position.

How can you deal with passive-aggressive people?

Place a priority on honesty and authenticity. Both require trust. If you don't build trust with people, they will usually become defensive, which drives them into passive-aggressiveness.

Ask clarifying questions. "Are you sure you're not angry?" "Is there anything you'd like to talk about or settle before we move on?" You might assume everyone understands or hears what you say, but clarification is worth the effort.

Be direct. If subtle approaches don't result in change, you will need to get more direct, such as "I know you say everything is okay, but your quick responses (or silence) indicate the opposite to me. I want to talk this out, but if you insist what you're saying is how you're feeling, I'll take you at your word." When you call someone out on their passive-aggressiveness, you've respectfully let them know you notice what they're doing. You've invited accountability into the relationship. If they insist on continuing or you find out later that the person wasn't forthcoming, you can remind them of the opportunity you gave them to express themselves.

Rebels

You know who they are: the people who always push the limits or cross the line. They go just beyond where you're comfortable. Sometimes it feels as if they tauntingly hold one foot over the line to see how you'll respond. It affects others, too; some people get uncomfortable and withdraw, while others want to join the adventure. You begin to wonder how long it will be before your team goes rogue.

Rebels might be stepping over the line from your perspective, but God might not be yanking them back as quickly or as far as you'd prefer. On the positive side, rebels can bring new possibilities to the table. Their enthusiasm and willingness to try new things can generate a lot of excitement and energy. Without rebels, many changes would never have happened. What seems like the norm now likely wasn't the norm years or decades ago. Someone took a risk to make a change. When you serve alongside rebels, you will have a front-row seat to some outstanding energy and ideas.

When you do have to rein in a rebel, avoid the role of rule-setter or police officer. Dealing with rebels requires building an authentic and trustworthy relationship with them (relationships again!). That gives you a say in their lives. At some point you'll have an opportunity to encourage them to apply the gifts and talents God has given them—in appropriate and helpful ways.

Handling prickly people doesn't mean you fix everything nor do the convicting. That's God's job, and he's good at it. He might use you, but it's still his responsibility, and only he knows the perfect timing and path. Building relationships and showing respect are the keys to unlocking God's power and grace in the lives of your co-laborers in God's kingdom.

"Don't just pretend to love others. Really love them. Hate what is wrong. Hold tightly to what is good. Love each other with genuine affection, and take delight in honoring each other. Never be lazy, but work hard and serve the Lord enthusiastically. Rejoice in our confident hope. Be patient in trouble, and keep on praying. When God's people are in need, be ready to help them. Always be eager to practice hospitality.

"Bless those who persecute you. Don't curse them; pray that God will bless them. Be happy with those who are happy, and weep with those who weep. Live in harmony with each other. Don't be too proud to enjoy the company of ordinary people. And don't think you know it all!

"Never pay back evil with more evil. Do things in such a way that everyone can see you are honorable. Do all that you can to live in peace with everyone."

—Romans 12:9-18

By Susan Lawrence

MATTHEW 18 IN THE REAL WORLD

"Bob" was known to be a quiet man who loved God. That's why everyone was surprised when he started accusing the worship pastor of giving him "an inappropriate hand gesture" in the hallway between Sunday morning services. This didn't seem credible on any level, but it was a serious accusation—one that the pastor had to address immediately.

Situations like this are common in churches, and there are no limits to the types of disputes that may arise between church members. Financial disagreements, personality clashes, parent/teacher issues, personal wrongs, and general relational discord are just a few of the probable and potential problems. Even the most diligent leader cannot have a contingency plan for every possible scenario. What a pastor can and should do, however, is internalize a set of biblical principles that can serve as a roadmap for dealing with many of these disputes.

See the "Pastor as Problem-Solver" chapter in this book for guidelines of when *not* to intervene.

1. Seek God's Guidance

God has provided much biblical wisdom for Christians to live together in peace. Pastors must cultivate a life of prayer and study, along with a biblical worldview that consistently leads him or her to God for direction on important matters. In the case of church conflict, pastors can find help by using the entirety of Matthew 18 as a guide for moderating the disputes that come their way.

2. Be Humble (Matthew 18:1-5)

Matthew 18:1 begins with the disciples asking Jesus how to become "great" in the kingdom. In response, Jesus referred to a child and said, "Anyone who becomes as humble as this little child is the greatest in the Kingdom of Heaven."

If you are to be effective in managing or mediating conflict, then you must approach those involved with genuine humility. Humility means not thinking you are better than other people, "the absence of pride or self-assertion," according to Webster's New World College Dictionary (4th edition). It's important to come out from behind the desk, sit alongside the parties involved, and present yourself as a fellow traveler on this difficult journey called life. This involves slowing down and listening intently, sincerely, and patiently to all sides. The initial goal is not simply to understand the facts but also to seek to understand the emotions involved for each party. Acknowledge their feelings, and sincerely seek to understand why they feel the way they do. Sincerely attempt to imagine how you might feel in the same situation.

3. Value These People (Matthew 18:6-9)

Jesus next warned about doing harm, whether intentional or accidental. More than a few pastors have done irreparable harm to an individual for the sake of "the church as a whole." Early in a dispute, pastors must remind themselves that the church is the people, that the individuals sitting in front of you are the church, too, and that these people matter. Seek their good. The win-win situation is for those involved to acknowledge one another's feelings and to agree to actively love each other regardless of how the specifics of the issue turn out. The central focus in any mediation is always the protection and preservation of relationships.

> The win-win situation is for those involved to acknowledge one another's feelings and to agree to actively love each other regardless.

4. Protect the Mission (Matthew 18:12-14)

There is a tension here that we must embrace. Negative, unhappy people are noisy, and because "the squeaky wheel gets the grease," pastors may feel they have to "grease" these squeakers. The result is that most churches are programmed according to the likes and dislikes of the most negative people. And yet, Jesus reminded his followers that God is most interested in finding and rescuing lost people.

MATTHEW 18 IN
THE REAL WORLD

Thus, while seeking to resolve disputes with all relationships intact, pastors must not lose sight of the mission to bring lost sheep into the fold. Avoid the pressure to give in to whatever silences the squeaky wheels if it weakens missional effectiveness. Look for ways to resolve conflict in a way that brings glory to God and helps the church achieve its mission.

5. Encourage Them to Talk (Matthew 18:15)

Jesus instructed his followers to go directly to the person who has wronged them. For pastors, this means that people need to be encouraged to speak directly to one another. Sometimes it can be helpful if a pastor sits in on the discussion. Much like in marital counseling, you might be able to help the individuals open up to each other in a safe environment.

6. Involve Others (Matthew 18:16)

As the conversation progresses, a pastor should involve others who are connected relationally to the people involved. These individuals can provide perspective and credibility to the process.

7. Pursue More Official Channels (Matthew 18:17)

For some conflicts, the governing body of the church may have to become involved. The goal is still the successful resolution of the conflict, with all parties walking away with relationships intact and the church still on course with its mission.

8. Power Up (Matthew 18:17-18)

In a healthy church with a culture of love and grace, few conflicts should reach this stage. But if some disputes prove especially difficult, the leadership of the church will need to provide the parties with clear, authoritative instructions regarding next steps. This should be done in a calm, loving, kind, yet firm manner. Pastors should never move to this stage alone. This should only be done in the context of a plurality of spiritual leaders, so as to avoid abuse of power. This step is biblical and occasionally necessary. The pastor or church that consistently "powers up" on its members, however, is creating a culture of spiritual abuse.

9. Love and Forgive (Matthew 18:17, 21-35)

Jesus said that if a brother won't listen to the leadership, "treat them as you would a pagan or a corrupt tax collector." Strictly understood, this means that the person in the wrong is no longer a member in good standing of the local congregation. But dig deeper. According to the totality of Jesus' example and Paul's instructions, how exactly are Christians supposed to treat pagans and tax collectors? With love! Christians are called to love their fellow believers, their neighbors, and even their enemies. Paul admonished Christians to "do everything with love" (1 Corinthians 16:14), and Jesus said that love is to be our distinguishing quality (John 13:34).

The application is that even when a dispute is unresolvable and church leadership is forced to bring official discipline to a situation, discipline should be administered with loving intent. To underscore this concept, Jesus told the story of the unmerciful servant, reminding his followers of the vast sin debt that has been cancelled on their behalf. He admonished all to never forget the gift they've received when dealing with others.

> Even when a dispute is unresolvable and church leadership is forced to bring official discipline to a situation, discipline should be administered with loving intent.

It turned out that Bob's behavior stemmed from his unhappiness with the direction of the music ministry. During the mediation process, he was unwilling to compromise or cooperate and encouraged the worship pastor to "find other employment." Bob was lovingly and firmly instructed to stop his divisive speech. Unfortunately, he did not and ended up leaving the church.

People questioned the pastor, expressing their concern and opinions about Bob's case. However, because these principles had been followed, no further damage was done to relationships, the church was able to continue its mission, and a spirit of peace prevailed.

By Brian Walton

PRACTICAL STUFF FOR PASTORS:
DEALING WITH CONFLICT

OWNING AND OVERCOMING CONFLICT

Leading a church is an unpredictable vocation. You never know when a phone call or drop-in visitor will renovate your schedule beyond recognition. But a few constants remain in ministry, one of which, unfortunately, is conflict. Although pastors are called to manage and mediate many conflicts between other people, they sometimes find themselves as one of the combatants. How you respond and resolve your personal conflicts will go a long way toward modeling how your congregation will deal with their own conflicts. Use this five-step process to help you navigate conflict well:

Assess It

First, define the issue to see if you can overlook this offense without falling into the trap of conflict avoidance. Briefly describe the conflict in writing. Then ask yourself:

- If I don't address the conflict, will there be an emotional wedge between me and the other person?

- Will God's or another person's reputation be damaged if I don't address the conflict?

If the answers to *both* questions is no, feel free to drop the matter.

Resolve and Reframe the Conflict

If you can't legitimately drop the issue, you need to deal with the conflict. Unfortunately, your amygdala—the part of your brain responsible for managing danger—famously has two responses: fight or flight. Neither will serve you well. Resolve to calmly address the skirmish before it grows into something larger. Instead of seeing the conflict as a source of danger, reframe it as an opportunity to gain greater clarity and closer relationship with the other person.

Own Your Piece of the Conflict

An offended person swiftly remodels his mind into a courtroom and puts his opponent on trial, usually at the expense of recognizing his own role in the conflict.

Roger Connors, Tom Smith, and Craig Hickman write in *The Oz Principle*, "To establish ownership, then, you must have the heart to tell both sides of the story, linking what you have done or failed to do with your current circumstances. Such a shift in perspective requires that you replace your victim story with an accountable one."[1]

Answer these questions to help you accurately see your part in the dispute:

- Have I repeatedly been in the same fight with different people?

- If the other person fought like me, how would I feel?

- Did I let the situation fester before engaging it?

- When I retell the story in my mind, what parts am I leaving out?

If the answer to any of these questions is unflattering, confess it to God and the other person(s).

Resolve It

In Matthew 18:15-17, Jesus gives the "how" of conflict resolution. He advocated using as little force as possible. The first step is to talk with the person in private—just between the two of you. Privacy creates safety, dignity, and a gracious environment in which to do the hard work of peacemaking.

If the two of you can't get on the same page, find a third party to help break the stalemate. Seek out a mature, unbiased person to help both of you work through the issues and police the quality of the communication in reaching a healthy, biblical resolution. Your church government might prescribe who that third party should be, oftentimes an elder. Whoever it is, make sure this person is respected and trusted by both parties to ensure the likelihood of success.

The final stage is the most intrusive. If you can't be reconciled with a mediator, the conflict is told "to the church," usually the governing board. The goal remains restoration. However, at this phase, the parties at odds begin to lose their freedom to negotiate and are subject to the prescriptions of the governing body.

Jesus' way is simple to describe but hard to practice. Beware of these unhealthy conflict patterns:

Triangulation: Call it venting, problem solving, or sharing a prayer request; but whenever we draw someone new (other than a mediator) into the dispute, we unnecessarily weave the conflict deeper into the congregation.

Non-verbal sparring: Healthy conflict *needs* good back-and-forth conversation, but it must be in person. Shun letters, email, or voice mail; written words are easily misinterpreted. Personal encounters allow for deeper understanding because tone of voice and facial and body expressions communicate in ways that other methods can't.

Grandstanding: Don't fight in front of an audience. It can subtly shift your goal from peacemaking to point scoring. If you find yourself on the wrong end of someone's grandstanding, listen without defending yourself. Acknowledge valid points.

Finish It

Don't make and accept apologies too early. Working through a dispute stirs up deep anxieties and other negative emotions, so it's tempting to declare the conflict over before you've actually finished the work. Before you shake hands, ask yourself:

- **Have I said the final 10 percent?** It's relatively easy to say 90 percent of what is bothering you in a disagreement. However, root issues, questions over motives, and spiritual concerns reside in the final 10 percent. Those topics are the hardest for us to address, so we settle for "speaking [some] of the truth in love." However, imagined-away fault lines still have the potential to rupture relationships and organizations the next time the conflict surfaces.

- **Did I listen?** Depending on your personality, it might be difficult for you to speak your peace well. But even if you do, your work is only half done. If you haven't taken the time to truly hear the other side of the story, odds are you've merely inflicted your "victim story" on the other party.

- **Did I restore the relationship?** Following the confrontation, make sure you maintain contact with the other individual. Ask if he or she needs to air anything. Perhaps you did some damage of your own during the disagreement. Never forget that the goal is reconciliation rather than victory.

OWNING AND OVERCOMING CONFLICT

If any of these questions points out a need to finish a conflict you've recently tried to resolve, start over. Cutting relational corners and placating might create emotional relief, but it's a fragile peace that will crumble.

You can handle conflict well if you arm yourself with the knowledge that it will be hard work and will sometimes drain you to the core. But remember, conflict is not an interruption to your ministry; it's another pathway toward becoming more like Jesus.

By Larry Shallenberger

What Is Your Default Conflict Style?

Avoidance—Ignores, disregards, or postpones the issue.

Positives: Dodges trouble, at least in the short term. Helpful if conflict is not really important.

Negatives: Unresolved problems and resentment usually resurface in time.

Competition—Win at all costs or at the expense of others.

Positives: Fast and efficient when one person gets his or her way.

Negatives: If one person wins, others must lose. Can offend and hurt others.

Accommodate—Put others' needs first or concede your needs entirely.

Positives: Can keep the peace, especially if the issue is truly unimportant to one party.

Negatives: The unmet needs of one party can erode respect.

Compromise—Seeks small wins and small concessions, "splitting the difference."

Positives: Helpful if the issue is complex.

Negatives: Some needs on both sides remain unmet.

Collaborate—Discuss and problem solve until mutually beneficial outcome is reached.

Positives: Creates mutual trust and open relationships.

Negatives: Takes time, energy, and participation by all parties.

REDEMPTIVE CONFLICT RESOLUTION

Unresolved conflict poisons everything. Restoration and reconciliation miraculously change everything.

True story: Two brothers live in the same small town and attend the same church. On Sunday mornings, the two choose to sit on opposite sides of the aisle, refusing to talk or even look at each other. Their estrangement began with an accusation followed by an intense argument. Lacking resolution, anger and bitterness set in. In a matter of days, nearly everyone in the church had formed an opinion and chosen a side of the church on which to sit. Forty-two years later the division remains, but few people can remember how or why it began.

Conflict in its early stages seems too tiny to be harmful. The offended person decides to avoid confrontation. Grace and peace appear to prevail. However, below the surface two realities exist: 1) the unresolved conflict can rapidly mutate into internal anger, bitterness, hatred, and an undetected desire for revenge; 2) the offender may continue to cause emotional, mental, and spiritual harm to others. The best treatment for this condition is face-to-face, honest conversation.

Many church leaders find these conversations to be difficult, stressful, and emotionally draining. Thankfully, Matthew 18:15-17 outlines a simple plan for dealing with conflict between Christians. The process begins with a personal meeting in a private setting. If the one who sinned (or is accused of sinning) refuses to admit wrongdoing, one or two unbiased witnesses should hear both sides. If the witnesses agree that someone has sinned and is unwilling to repent, the church must be informed. If the person remains unmoved by the direction provided by the church, then he or she would be dismissed from this church.

> For more details on this scriptural approach, see the "Matthew 18 in the Real World" chapter in this book.

Personal Conflict in the Church

Any time two or more people spend significant time together, friction is bound to occur. When interpersonal friction reaches a certain point, the smoldering embers burning deep in one's memory have the potential to become a raging forest fire.

People also deal with stress and pressure in a variety of ways. Ministry pressure can come from many different places and makes itself visible in many forms. In times of stress, people can turn against one another rather than working together in a supportive relationship. When conflict occurs, an effective approach is to evaluate the pressures that are upon everyone involved and respond in ways that glorify God and edify the body of Christ.

A Redemptive Approach to Personal Conflict

"Do all that you can to live in peace with everyone" (Romans 12:18). While this may be more difficult in particular situations, this biblical principle should be the goal of all Christians. Jesus prayed for all believers by saying, "I pray that they will all be one, just as you and I are one—as you are in me, Father, and I am in you. And may they be in us so that the world will believe you sent me" (John 17: 21). Unity, not conflict, is the desire of the Lord. Christian leaders should approach every conflict with a redemptive approach. A redemptive approach includes the following principles:

1. Be proactive. Recognize when staff and other leaders possess diverse perspectives, strengths, and personality types that may lead to conflict.

Listen from the posture of a fellow Christian who has been rescued by Christ, with humility and grace.

2. Listen first. The willingness to listen will often determine the outcome of any given situation. Not all listening is equal, however. An attitude of "I would never have done that" shows you to be judgmental and quick to condemn. A better approach is one of humility and grace, as a fellow Christian who has been rescued by Christ.

3. Use the Bible as a guide. When addressing the issue of sin with someone else, we are not appealing to our own judgments or moral standards, but only to that which God has clearly defined in his Word.

4. Recognize the condition of the person's heart and greatest need. It is easy to point to social vices and external habits that repulse us. While we cannot easily see the heart of another, we can attempt to know someone and their struggle before discerning the sin. Through conversation, we should seek to discover any unmet expectations and talk about them.

5. Provide a concrete plan for restoration after prayer and consultation with other church leaders. Meeting with someone face to face is the first step. An appropriate second step is for church leaders to spend time in prayer. Then a simple, direct restoration plan should be proposed that provides clear action steps and consequences for everyone involved.

A redemptive approach to personal conflict maintains a focus on restoration. The growth of a Christian is halted when he or she refuses to turn away from sin. The foremost concern is the restoration of a believer's fellowship with the Lord Jesus. Sin and its relational impact is also a threat to the church community. Intervening can be messy and difficult, but neglecting this leadership role is far more devastating to the individuals and the church.

A redemptive approach to personal conflict maintains a focus on restoration.

When Conflict Goes Public

There may be rare situations when information must come before the entire church. While leaders should exhaust other means of restoration before this occurs, sometimes the sin of an individual must be revealed publicly. A few guidelines should be considered when this becomes necessary.

First, the behavior must be clearly defined in Scripture as sinful for *all* people. For example, the church should not discipline a member for watching a particular television show, but would be right to discipline someone who is unrepentant after stealing a television (because we have a clear and universal command from God not to steal).

Second, church discipline must be for specific behaviors. For example, a member should not be disciplined for lacking kindness. One *can* be disciplined for abusing his wife without any remorse for his action.

Last, in disclosing information about a member's misconduct, church leaders must be careful with legal and ethical issues. Have a written policy regarding church discipline and confidentiality that all members know. Keep detailed notes on every conflict so that if the church fellowship becomes involved, only verifiable facts can be communicated. And do not share information with anyone uninvolved in the process.

The Power of Reconciliation

Remember the two brothers at the beginning of this chapter who turned a church and town into a place of division and mistrust? Their feud began over a simple property dispute. The brothers built their homes side by side. One put up a fence, and the two disagreed on the exact property line. Long ago, the fence rotted away. The feud, however, set the course for generations. Sadly, some churches have a story like this, too.

Because we have been restored in a relationship with God, we can have a ministry of reconciliation with others. Leaders of God's church should extend the same grace to others as God has given us. When we do, Christ is glorified, and people see his redemptive story in action. "Your love for one another will prove to the world that you are my disciples" (John 13:35).

By Jeremy Amick

THE PASTOR AS PROBLEM-SOLVER

A woman in the church complains that a nursery volunteer was rude.

A deacon is upset that he wasn't invited to sing in the men's quartet.

Two teenage boys aren't getting along, and it's causing tension between the parents.

An older man complains every Sunday that the worship music is too loud.

Inevitably, every pastor is called upon to help solve problems that arise among the people they lead. According to the U.S. Congregational Life Survey, 8 out of 10 pastors reported conflict within their church in the past two years.[2] When Christians at various phases of spiritual maturity are placed in close proximity to one another over a period of time, conflict is certain to arise. Pastors would do well to stop being surprised at this reality and begin to engage it as an opportunity.

Perhaps, counterintuitively, pastors should not see their role as avoiding or resolving all conflicts that develop between people in the church. While it is certainly necessary for leaders to engage with some situations, the role of "Supreme Solver of All Problems" should be intentionally resisted. Those leaders who take on such a role will eventually be distracted from their primary mission, discouraged by negativity, and perhaps worst of all, will deprive their people of an important path toward spiritual growth.

Staying on Mission

It is impossible to create a list of priorities that holds true for every pastor. And yet, a model can be helpful.

A pastor is first and foremost a follower of Christ. Based on that core identity, other roles and responsibilities can revolve around it:

- A pastor is a leader and vision-caster.
- A pastor is a preacher of God's Word.
- A pastor is an equipper of people.
- A pastor must be a faithful steward.

The Pastor on Mission

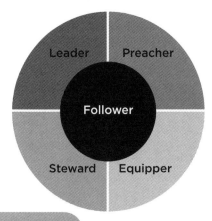

Leader

Preacher

Follower

Steward

Equipper

If pastors consistently allow themselves to be drawn into the problems that develop between people, mediation and problem solving will soon be all they do. They will find themselves "holding court" on a daily basis, hearing disputes, and dispensing justice. It is important to be aware of this because this is more tempting than anyone cares to admit. There is something enticing about being called upon to exercise authority and demonstrate wisdom. Many great leaders unwittingly fall into this mode, seduced by the sense of self-importance and purpose that accompany such roles.

The Bible says that "Moses took his seat to hear the people's disputes against each other. They waited before him from morning till evening" (Exodus 18:13). Imagine long lines of people waiting all day to tell Moses about property disputes and various personal conflicts. They depended on Moses for direction, and their helplessness bolstered and solidified Moses' importance as their leader, although he apparently found this daily scenario exhausting.

Moses' father-in-law, Jethro, responded in a straightforward manner: "This is not good!" (Exodus 18:17). He coached Moses to be a better steward of his time and leadership by equipping others and encouraging them to become more independent. Jethro's advice was on point for Moses, and it certainly ought to be heeded by those who serve the church today.

Jesus mediated a new covenant and has given all people equal access to God. Whatever the case may have been for Moses and the people of Israel, the situation for God's people today is indisputable. They don't need to come to their pastor to know God's will. They need to be equipped and encouraged to go to God. To put yourself as an obstacle between the people and God—even if unintentionally—is detrimental to them and to you.

The primary role of the pastor as disciple-maker is to equip God's people (Ephesians 4:12). Similar to effective parenting, effective pastoral care leads people toward independence, not dependence. This involves teaching them to interpret and apply the Word for themselves, as well as leading them to resolve their own problems and conflicts. Sometimes a mother must resist the urge to intervene and let her children learn how to work things out among themselves.

Pastors must invest themselves in the development of leaders and should model the 2:2:2 principle: "Now teach these truths to other trustworthy people who will be able to pass them on to others" (2 Timothy 2:2). This relational process will require your time and energy on behalf of emerging leaders, rather than in settling a never-ending series of squabbles and disputes. The effort given to leadership development will more than make up later for any short-term deficit of attention to solving every problem the church has.

The more responsibility a pastor has, the fewer decisions he should make—but the more consequential those decisions will likely be.

There will still be issues that you need to deal with, but these should be fewer and farther between. The more responsibility a pastor has, the fewer decisions he should make—but the more consequential those decisions will likely be. Deciding when to engage a situation or not is a judgment call, but here are a few questions to ask before putting on the problem-solving hat:

- Have the individuals talked? You should rarely engage in a conflict if those involved have not

  See the "Matthew 18 in the Real World" and "Redemptive Conflict Resolution" chapters in this book for more details on this issue.

  followed Matthew 18 and already attempted resolution. When hearing a complaint for the first time, you should always ask, "Have you gone to this person and told them what you just told me?"

- Is this a sin issue or a personality issue? The reality is that some people are oil, and others are water. Christians are called to love one another, but they won't all become close friends. If sin is involved, pastoral counsel and mediation may be called for. Personality conflicts need not be.

- Does this involve biblical principles or preferences? Pastors will never win if personal preferences (theirs or others') prevail in the culture of the church. Therefore, pastors must teach their people how to distinguish between biblical principles and personal preferences.

Conflict Can Be Healthy

Proverbs 27:17 tells us, "As iron sharpens iron, so a friend sharpens a friend." This verse refers to the benefits of human friendship, but it also implies the inevitable friction that accompanies human interactions. Iron cannot sharpen iron unless the two pieces are placed in close proximity over time. By design, human beings have an impact on one another at a deep level. This is one of the ways God brings about transformation in a human life.

Consider that among the disciples was Simon the Zealot and Matthew the tax collector. Zealots were an impassioned political party who hated the Roman government and desired to see it overthrown. The only people Zealots hated more than Romans were Jews who were Roman sympathizers and collaborators—such as tax collectors. Do you think there might have been some conflict between those two? And to think Jesus picked them to do life with each other! He must have known that these two men could learn from each other in relationship. No doubt he used that to help them fully become who they were created to be.

By Brian Walton

THE RIGHT WAY TO FIGHT

You're not doing something right.

If you aren't sure what it is, ask anyone in your church. Even your biggest fan likely disagrees with you about something. Just be prepared to hear it raw and unfiltered.

A volunteer may share a hard critique right after you've poured your heart out and feel vulnerable. A staff member will unfairly challenge you in a meeting. An anonymous note will randomly demand changes you must make. Emails will show up in your inbox tomorrow questioning something you said today.

You'll feel undermined, challenged, and judged. You'll run out of strategy. You'll be tempted to choose between being proven right or silently suffering the accusations.

All while reminding yourself that it's absolutely worth it.

Conflict Is Biblical

The New Testament church was not homogenous. Jesus' original disciples came from various levels of society. When their numbers grew into the thousands, the first Christians soon started complaining about being mistreated:

As the believers rapidly multiplied, there were rumblings of discontent. The Greek-speaking believers complained about the Hebrew-speaking believers, saying that their widows were being discriminated against in the daily distribution of food. So the Twelve called a meeting of all the believers. (Acts 6:1-2)

Soon after this episode, there was major disagreement over who could and could not join the ranks of this new movement (see Acts 15). And later, there was this embarrassing incident when a veteran leader was put in his place by a newer leader: "When Peter came to Antioch, I had to oppose him to his face, for what he did was very wrong" (Galatians 2:11).

John 16:33 records Jesus clearly proclaiming that we should expect trouble in the world. This apparently includes within the church, as it isn't yet perfected as it will be in eternity. Still, we do have the same means to address conflict as we do anything else in life: by putting Jesus Christ first in all things.

Perspectives and Focal Points

If the original disciples challenged Jesus and each other, don't be surprised when Christians idealize their personal perspective over God's or yours. Although they may know how to deal with conflict at home or on the job, what works in those settings may not always succeed in the church. Even when Matthew 18 is used as a formula for conflict resolution, it may not yield the results you expect. This model is not inherently designed for conflict resolution but for confronting sin. Differences in personality types or leadership styles are not, in and of themselves, religious or moral issues.

Instead, imagine an unhealthy church culture as though it were a mountain of conflict. Its top layer embodies a noticeable scandal of sin, and the bottom layer embodies common personality issues. As people justifiably feel hurt by the actual sin and its consequences, personality issues could factor in but would seem comparatively less important (or less noticeable, at least).

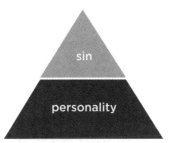

Now imagine a church that has no outrageous sin that is evident. The top layer of deliberate sin doesn't exist. This leaves the next layer down—the personality mix—to become the new, reshaped mountain. This becomes the focus of conflict, even though it doesn't fall into moral or ethical categories. But it can *appear* to be immoral, simply by default. If people do something you disagree with, you will assume it to be unfair or unjust when it may simply be a personality difference. And so the conflict begins.

The better option is to make Jesus the high point of your congregation's attention. Mission statements and policy manuals can declare it, but your core leadership must live it. People are going to talk about and focus on something, so give them something worth talking about and focusing on.

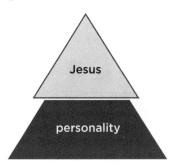

Proactive and Reactive Processes

It's ironic that the very God-given institution we fight within is the one God designed to bring peace into the world. Still, a commitment to work things out can freshly reveal the reconciling love, power, and presence of Jesus Christ. According to Ken Sande, founder of Peacemaker Ministries, "As we draw on his grace, follow his example, and put his teachings into practice, we can find freedom from the impulsive, self-centered decisions that make conflict worse, and bring praise to God by displaying the power of the gospel in our lives."[3]

- **Begin with vision.** Remind others about who God says we're able to become and the mission in which God has invited us to participate. People are more likely to abandon fights over trivial matters if they know what's important.

- **Champion prayerful consensus.** Instead of voting on everything, pray about the issue until all parties reach a general unity. Help people realize that loud opinions are not as important as God's whisper. Whenever possible, drop the cultural idea to "agree to disagree," and instead agree to honor Christ by working things out.

- **Ooze grace.** Overlook everything offensive except for sin. Even then, look to restore people into their future rather than label them according to their pasts.

- **Assert what matters.** Know the handful of values you'll live by, and then die to yourself on everything else.

- **Make space for disagreement.** Have an open-door policy for people to give input on big ideas before they're launched.

THE RIGHT WAY TO FIGHT

- **Don't squelch tension.** Let volunteer and staff leaders work things out themselves. Wait to speak a few words to help redirect things as necessary.

  See "The Pastor as Problem-Solver" chapter in this book for more tips on this point.

- **Diversify leadership.** Don't have an entire team composed of paid staff members. Invite mature volunteers to speak into key meetings, not as mavericks but to foster communication and mutual accountability.

- **Map out conflict.** Identify everything that contributed to a disagreement. Consider past history, differing personalities, personal values, worldview, a fear of public perception, and any personal need for validation. Today's issue may be more about how someone hasn't let go of yesterday's troubles. You *can* overcome this.

- **Write awkward notes only when necessary.** Do as much as you can in person. If you have to write a letter or email, compose it three times and walk away from it in between rewrites. Stick to the topic and affirm the relationship with the person.

- **Declare the hand-off.** Clarify who gets the final decision rights on the issue. Whenever appropriate, give it away to the other person.

- **Don't bring it home.** Spare your family from seeing someone you're at odds with through a negative lens. Only ask for general prayer, avoiding specifics.

- **Develop a process for mediation.** Define when and how you'll seek outside help, whether from within your denomination or through a neighboring church.

As you read through the Gospels, you'll notice that Jesus invited personality squabbles into his inner circle through the people he recruited. Take note of what he did and didn't care about as you navigate what you should and shouldn't care about. Assume the best of intentions from others, evaluating your part in the conflict, owning what you need to own, and resisting evil along the way.

By Tony Myles

THE RIGHT WAY TO FIGHT

HANDLING FINANCIAL CONFLICTS

Money, the proverbial root of all evil, creates perpetual problems in God's church. Problems arise from misunderstandings with donors, their expectations, and transparency. Churches invite trouble when they overlook best practices with their treasurers and financial leaders. Arguments happen when the church's vision, staff expectations, and budgetary realities are inconsistent. All the while, the Bible warns that money destroys when it is loved, but blesses when it is given with a generous heart.

Conflicts With Donors

Donor confidence rests on the church's ability to hold itself to a higher standard than what is legally required. The builder generation (born between 1901 and 1925) has sacrificed and saved. They expect their church to handle their money as conservatively as they have. Younger donors, especially millennials (born between 1980 and 2000), demand a high level of transparency in church finances. They view the church as skeptically as they do government and big business. Unfortunately, the church has earned this skepticism, so trust must be earned rather than presumed.

Help avoid any tendencies toward secrecy by clearly displaying financial integrity. Have a yearly audit and freely communicate the results. A successful audit is a reason to celebrate and generates confidence. Not everyone (except accountant types) will get excited about financial details, but hiding finances is sure to create a breeding ground for suspicion. Think of dollars as votes; donors vote for transparency.

> Hiding finances is sure to create a breeding ground for suspicion. Think of dollars as votes; donors vote for transparency.

A donation implies a complete release of all interest in a gift with no strings attached. In general, then, a charitable gift should not be refunded. If a change in expenditures is required, most donors will tolerate it if they feel that the decision has been prayerfully considered and the reason for the change has been communicated well. But some donors might ask questions such as, "Why would we build a new gymnasium when we need a new kitchen so badly?" When questions like this arise, it's likely that the vision of the church has been poorly communicated.

Other times, churches abandon projects. You might raise a sum of money for parking lot repair only to experience roof failure. Donors to the parking lot project may become upset when the money is diverted to an alternative project. The cure is to place as few restrictions as possible on fundraising goals and to have clear backup plans and options.

A simple "thank you" to donors develops relationships and avoids conflict. You can thank your regular donors with one generic letter, enclosed with a year-end charitable contribution statement. Expressing gratitude verbally in between these yearly letters will further improve donor relationships.

Conflicts With Money Handlers

Churches are unique environments of trust. Volunteers who receive and count the offering or serve as treasurers are chosen because they seem to be competent and honest. This trust can lead churches to compromise sound money management.

One church wisely had a written policy that required offerings to be counted immediately by at least two unrelated persons and immediately deposited. In practice, the church allowed a senior couple—long time trusted members—to take the money home and count it and deposit it the next morning. When a new pastor asked about correcting this practice, the lay leaders responded, "We know the rules because we wrote them. But they were not written for brother and sister Jones! We trust them!"

Thankfully there was no fraud; however, the church failed to protect the Joneses and itself from the perception of risk. Every church should occasionally evaluate their money handling practices, from the moment of collection to the payment of invoices. Ask two questions: 1) Are we handling money so as to avoid conflict? 2) Are we handling money so as to avoid the *perception* of conflict?

Sometimes church treasurers become irrationally possessive of funds. Once personal opinions begin to guide the flow of money, conflict is bound to develop. The cure is a proper understanding of roles in the money-handling process. Financial overseers should function in machine-like fashion. Their role is to present correct and complete information and to carry out instructions from the appropriate leaders. Whether they agree with a particular expenditure is irrelevant.

The king of church financial conflicts is fraud. In nearly every case of fraud there is a triangular relationship between opportunity (relaxed practices), perceived need, and rationalization on the part of the offender. One treasurer, with access to pre-deposit cash (opportunity), didn't have her wallet at the grocery store (need). She borrowed from the night deposit bag, planning to return it later (rationalization). As often happens in cases of embezzlement, her illegal behavior escalated in frequency and volume.

Churches must put in place safeguards to avoid even the appearance of impropriety. In a small church, a young pastor asked his wife, an experienced accountant, to count the money. She was reluctant to take on this role but agreed when they could find no one else to assume the responsibility. Soon, the congregation was whispering. Why was the pastor's wife wearing new clothes and fancy jewelry? Was she skimming money from the offering plate? The pastor immediately ordered an audit, which showed that his wife had followed proper accounting procedures. But the pastor's poor judgment in assigning his wife the financial responsibilities of the church eroded the confidence of the congregation and proved to be his undoing. The rumors were too widespread, and the pastor eventually resigned his position.

Church fraud is ugly. Although restoration and forgiveness may occasionally occur, it will always involve embarrassment and hurt. You can prevent fraud by providing an unsuitable environment for it. Audits can show that accounting procedures are being followed, but audits rarely expose fraud. Fraud is more typically exposed via a tip or the observance of peculiar behavior. Be rigid in following best practices, minimize opportunities for fraud, and closely observe behavior.

Conflicts With the Budget

Many Christians, whether lay leaders or clergy, have a passion for ministry. One person's passion might be for children's ministry while another's is for compassionate ministry to the poor. Yet another's passion is for discipleship. Each ministry has value in the Lord's kingdom, but unless the church has unlimited resources, conflict can arise when ministry leaders have to fight for their funding. Reconciling these competing priorities will depend upon a shared vision.

A carefully prepared church budget, approved in advance, keeps the vision in focus and priorities in perspective. Without a budget, churches are inviting conflict over their limited financial resources. The dollars will flow toward the ministry which is represented by the most passionate promoter. This may be the most extroverted leader or even the one who asks first. A budget enables a church to engage in focused ministry, linking resources to vision.

> Without a budget, churches are inviting conflict over their limited financial resources...A budget enables a church to engage in focused ministry, linking resources to vision.

In churches, as in marriages, money can be a source of great blessing or a cause of great conflict. Conflict can occur when there is not enough of it, too much of it, or even about the right amount. Volume is irrelevant for matters of stewardship. God's expectation is that the church will care for its resources and use them wisely.

By Mark Lail

WHEN CONFLICT COMES CLOSE TO HOME

Can someone please reconcile Luke 14:26 and 1 Timothy 5:8 for me?

> If you want to be my disciple, you must hate everyone else by comparison—your father and mother, wife and children, brothers and sisters—yes, even your own life. Otherwise, you cannot be my disciple. (Luke 14:26)

> But those who won't care for their relatives, especially those in their own household, have denied the true faith. Such people are worse than unbelievers. (1 Timothy 5:8)

What is a pastor or ministry leader supposed to do with these passages? How do you strike the right balance between the demands of ministry and family responsibilities? According to the majority of research on pastors' personal lives, too many have not found that balance. Pastors report feeling isolated, burned out, and paralyzed by pressure that extends into their homes (see the following sidebar). And when pastors and their families fall, collateral damage is created for the churches they lead.

- 13% of pastors surveyed have had marriages that have fallen apart and ended in divorce

- 45% have experienced depression or burnout to the degree of needing a leave of absence

- 56% of pastor's wives say they have no close friends

- 80% believe pastoral ministry affects their families negatively

- 66% of pastors and their families feel pressure to model the perfect, ideal family to their congregation.[4]

God's Greatest Gift... Christian Community

It's sadly ironic that church leaders often don't live in Christian community. Isolating themselves from the congregation ignores the gift of a covenant community that God has given us. In their social networks, pastors need to have:

One Absolute Confidant: This is for personal accountability. Pastors need at least one non-family person who can be a sounding board. With this person they can confess sin, share struggles, express doubts, celebrate successes, or anything else that is best shared with someone in absolute trust.

A Close Group of Peers: This is for accountability for a life of worship and discipleship. Worship and discipleship are responses to what God has done; therefore all of life should be redirected toward our relationship with God. It is important to have in your life a group of friends who can check and encourage you to a life of absolute surrender.

Smaller Christian Community: This is for accountability at the family level. Pastoral families need to be linked to other Christian families. People need to see how pastors interact with their spouses, discipline and shepherd their children, and live out their faith around others.

> The roles and skill set necessary for leading a church are not necessarily appropriate at home.

Leading Your Family

You may have to be a different leader at home than you are at church. The roles and skill set necessary for leading a church are not necessarily the same as those appropriate at home. Your spouse needs a fully engaged partner. Your children need involved parents. You need a safe haven where you can be yourself.

This is not to say that your family can flourish in a leadership vacuum. I once heard a challenging question given to a room full of business leaders: "If you put the same energy into your family as you did your business, would it be possible for it to fail?" Your family needs you to bring the same vision, energy, and values to them that you bring to your ministry.

WHEN CONFLICT COMES CLOSE TO HOME

Here are two examples from my own life:

5x35. My wife and I each came up with five things we would like to do or see happen by the time we were 35 (we were 31 at the time). This list could be 4x40 or 6x60 or 2x52...the numbers can be personalized. Then we came up with goals and timelines for each. It was a way to focus our resources, time, and prayers toward those five dreams.

Create a family crest. We asked our children all the things they liked about our family and all of the things they would rather do without. We then asked them what was most important to our family as a whole. From those lists we came up with three values that we wanted to uphold in our family no matter what and made a "Family Crest" out of them, with the motto, "Be an Adventurer—Be the Solution—Be the Good News."

Combating Busyness

The key to overcoming the absent-when-home mentality is a fundamental redirection of energy and approach to life. Here are five tips that have helped me and may be helpful for you:

1. **Know it's coming.** Some seasons in Christian ministry and church calendars are busier than others. Awareness of these times is half the battle to combat busyness. Knowing it's coming before it arrives allows you to both prepare mentally and schedule a couple of guaranteed times—like Boy's Day or Date Night—

into the rare holes. Ask yourself, "Knowing my life is going to be a sprint for the next four weeks, what do I need to intentionally prepare so as not to outrun my family?"

2. More yes than no. When you are too busy, it's easy to feel that every request from your family becomes an extra burden. Whether it's your son asking to play basketball or your daughter asking you to take a walk, your automatic response is, "No." Track every time your kids ask you to do something and make sure that you have two "Yes's" for every "No."

3. Give them your best 15. Instead of immediately disconnecting from the world when you first get home, use the first 15 minutes after you get home to connect with your family. In addition, spend the last 15 minutes right before bed with them, too. It can make a huge impact. It will show them the value they have in your life when you give them your first, last, and best.

4. Bring them with you. Even if it's only once a week during a busy season, this practice will add five, six, or seven more times together. There are many added bonuses to this as well, such as your kids getting to see you at work, interacting with strangers, modeling behavior, etc. Get out your calendar and circle every event or appointment that your family could join, then ask them along.

5. Plug into the right outlet. We need a source of energy and will draw it from something. The busier we get, the more we default to drawing it from ourselves, which is a very limited source. Christians are intended to draw upon God, specifically the Holy Spirit, to fill us up. Find 15 minutes every day to plug directly into God's power and energy.

In our larger, Christian community, we need to be honest about the problems and challenges of balancing ministry and family and work together toward some solutions. Hopefully the ideas offered here can be some starting places so you don't miss one of your greatest opportunities to witness to our culture: the strength of our families.

By Austin Maxheimer

LEAVING WELL

It was rumored for months that the McLanes might leave the church. Their frustration with its imperfections only seemed to grow the more involved they became. Nothing could please them even though the senior pastor reached out multiple times to resolve the tension. The McLanes used these conversations to share their complaints and point fingers, never realizing their own negativity.

The McLanes would have told a different story. They felt a burden for the churchwide "math problem" of so much to do and not enough people stepping up to do it. It felt even more frustrating that Pastor Alan didn't give them complete autonomy to solve problems as they saw fit. They loved the church and its people but concluded church leadership was too controlling.

The McLanes ultimately decided to leave without notifying Pastor Alan. He found out anyway and asked to get together. They initially resisted but later agreed to meet if it wouldn't involve rehashing any of the issues. "The greatest thing that could happen at this point is good closure," the husband stated.

"Couldn't the greatest thing be for us to reconcile and move forward committed to each other?" Pastor Alan countered. "Isn't Jesus capable of doing that if we're all willing to let him lead us?"

"I prayed about it already," the husband replied.
"Nothing is going to change us leaving. Let's just talk
about good closure."

Whose Church Is It?

Some people leave their congregations for reasons
that can't be faulted, such as a household relocation, a
debilitating physical challenge, or death itself. Others
depart because of theological differences or because of
genuinely sinful behavior by someone in leadership or
the congregation. However, most people seem to walk
away for reasons that they perceive as insurmountable
but actually are resolvable:

- Friction with members or leaders.

- Battles over worship service preferences.

- Comments on social media.

- Differences in politics.

- Embarrassment over home-life issues.

- Fainthearted commitments in others.

- Guilt from an inability or unwillingness to tithe.

- Having a family member who critiques the church.

The common element shared by these issues is the feeling
that they are an obstacle to what *I* want to experience in
my church. If only this matter could be addressed to *my*
liking, then I might be convinced to stay.

Most people seem to walk away for reasons that they perceive as insurmountable but actually are resolvable.

Many of these issues could be worked out by lifting up our heads and fixing our eyes on the true owner of the church. The Apostle Paul recognized this when he wrote to the conflict-ridden church in Corinth: "I am writing to God's church in Corinth" (1 Corinthians 1:2).

Seeing God as the church's owner helps us recognize that the church isn't merely a means for our self-expression or fulfillment, but a covenant community we belong to for God's glory. If we recognize this, we could avoid creating the divisions that the New Testament repeatedly rails against.

Unfortunately, someone who is disgruntled with the way church is being run or who is in conflict with another church member cannot see this larger picture. Blind spots might magnify the immediate issue over the big picture, elevating feelings over faithfulness. Unhappy people also surround themselves with other unhappy people, begetting a spiral of negativity. When people are emotionally exhausted in this way, they eventually sigh, "Enough is enough."

The Splash and the Ripples

Church exits affect everyone in the same way a large stone dropped into water creates a series of ripples that extend far beyond the initial splash. I watched this as one family left a church but continued causing trouble from the outside. The husband kept ducking direct requests for reconciliation and eventually emailed a trumped-up denouncement of the church's leadership to dozens of families. People who at first seemed neutral to the family's departure later used that email to justify their own exit when they experienced their own problems with the congregation. They received validation from others they'd connected with when the email occurred. The ripples still affected people years later.

Whether it is one person or multiple families leaving the church, pastors should be willing to engage the ripples left behind. Here are some key (usually unspoken) questions you can prepare to respond to when the time comes. Note the different questions that come from different groups of people, depending on their varying level of involvement. Note also the questions shared by all parties involved.

The people involved who are going	The people involved who are staying	The people not involved who are watching
Am I going to be chased?	Am I going to be alone?	Am I going to be next?
Should I keep any of my old friends?	Should I be unguarded in making new friends?	Should I take sides between my friends?
What *really* happened?	What *really* happened?	What *really* happened?
How do I start over?	How do I start over?	How do I start over?

Plan Z

If no compromise seems possible, those in conflict will have to determine if they will part ways amicably and graciously. Even in this, "closure" is not the primary goal; honoring Jesus and letting him redirect the process is.

- **Pray.** Don't skip this daily step or trivialize it by declaring, "I prayed about it." Prayer isn't a one-time activity to vent our frustrations about others, but to foster ongoing, God-led pliability in us.

- **Reaffirm your capital "C" church relationship.** Even Christians who aren't in a local congregation are still in a covenant relationship with God and each other. Consider sharing Communion together or some other act of Christian unity. Talk about practical, ongoing ways to further this.

- **Involve a mediator.** Identify someone spiritually mature who can keep things grounded and identify which lines (if any) need to be drawn.

- **Describe the exit.** Help everyone involved see the door and identify what it means. For example, is the exit about no longer attending weekend services or does it also affect events and relationships?

- **Create long-term language.** Establish what can be genuinely said to magnify Christ even years later when someone says, "Tell me what really happened." Begin this conversation now by claiming how you've significantly added to each other's lives and spiritual formation.

- **Be a ghost-buster.** When people leave a church, they leave behind a metaphorical "ghost." Their lack of presence eerily reminds others of when they were once alive there. Do some ghost-busting by honoring the person's impact and empowering others to further that legacy through new efforts and ideas.

- **Note secondary effects.** Recognize how everyday logistics will be effected when people leave. Alert your finance team to any financial impact the church may feel.

• **Own what can be changed.** Use this exit to prevent future losses by learning what was perceived on all sides and making appropriate changes.

Whether or not any of your actions help someone leave well, continually follow the Spirit of Christ. Abandon the desire to "win" or rally the troops against a common enemy (those leaving), as if you were in combat with them—because you are not. You are in service to the people of God's church, which is being built by Jesus Christ. Lead as if your church's life depended on *that* rather than any other human factor—because it does.

By Tony Myles

Endnotes

1. Roger Connors, Tom Smith, and Craig Hickman, *The Oz Principle: Getting Results Through Individual and Organizational Accountability* (Paramus, NJ: Prentice Hall Press, 1994), 127.

2. Deborah Bruce, "Congregational Conflict: Common or Uncommon?" *Beyond the Ordinary: Insights Into U.S. Congregational Life* (blog), *U.S. Congregational Life Survey*, March 20, 2012, http://www.uscongregations.org/beyond-the-ordinary/congregational-conflict-common-or-uncommon/.

3. Ken Sande, *The Peacemaker: A Biblical Guide to Resolving Personal Conflict* (Grand Rapids, MI: Baker, 2004), 12.

4. H.B. London, Jr. and Neil B. Wiseman, *Pastors at Greater Risk* (Ventura, CA: Regal Books, 2003), 86, 172, 118, 20, 148.